STRIDERS

Up in the Peaks

T0315958

Contents

SCHOLASTIC

Published in the UK by
Scholastic Education, 2024
Scholastic Distribution Centre, Bosworth Avenue,
Tournament Fields, Warwick, CV34 6UQ
Scholastic Ireland, 89E Lagan Road, Dublin
Industrial Estate, Glasnevin, Dublin, D11 HP5F

1 2 3 4 5 6 7 8 9   4 5 6 7 8 9 0 1 2 3

Printed by Ashford Colour Press

This book is made of materials from
well-managed, FSC®-certified forests
and other controlled sources.

MIX
Paper from
responsible sources
FSC® C011748

A CIP catalogue record for this book is available
from the British Library.

ISBN 978-0702-32727-8

Author
Rachel Russ

Editorial team
Rachel Morgan, Vicki Yates, Jane Jackson,
Alison Gilbert

Design team
Dipa Mistry, Andrea Lewis and We Are Grace

Photographs
Cover Gaurav Aryal/Shutterstock
p4–5 Kertu/Shutterstock
p5, 8, 9, 10, 11, 13, 14, 17,19, 20, 21, 23
(triangles) flovie/Shutterstock
p4–5,16,18 (circle border) Allies Interactive/
Shutterstock
p5, 20–21 Thampitakkull Jakkree/Shutterstock
p6–7 Daniel Prudek/Shutterstock
p7 (yak) Crazy nook/Shutterstock
p7 (griffon vulture) SIDDHARTH_TIWARI 36/
Shutterstock
p7 (marmot) AneeshKotwal/Shutterstock
p7 (ibex) David Havel/Shutterstock
p7, 9, 10, 13 (negative) 32 pixels/Shutterstock
p8–9 Teresa Bauer/Shutterstock
p9 (bird swooping) Zhecho Planinski/Shutterstock
p10 PhotocechCZ/Shutterstock
p4, 10–11 slowmotiongli/iStock
p5, 12–13 Ranjith_july/Shutterstock
p13 Wang LiQiang/Shutterstock
p14 Tsewang Gurmet/Shutterstock
p15 Ovchinnikova Irina/Shutterstock
p16 tahirsphotography/Shutterstock
p16–17 tahir abbas/iStock
p4, 18–19 CameraOnHand/Shutterstock
p18 Serge Goujon/Shutterstock
p21 (pattern) flovie/Shutterstock
p21, 23 (torn paper) klyaksun/Shutterstock
p21 hadynyah/iStock
p22–23 Joel Zahnd/Shutterstock
p23 (children carrying baskets) Berzina/
Shutterstock
p24 (sky) VittoriaChe/Shutterstock

How to use this book

This book practises these letters and letter sounds:

ay (as in 'ways')	ou (as in 'found')
ea (as in 'eat')	u (as in 'human')

Here are some of the words in the book that use the sounds above:

stay   around   peaks   humans

This book uses these common tricky words:

**the   are   to   of   there   little   here
be   something   they   like   by   have**

Before reading

- Read the title and look at the cover. Discuss what this book might be about.

During reading

- If necessary, sound out and then blend the sounds to read the word: p-ea-k-s, peaks.
- Pause every so often to talk about the information.

After reading

- Talk about what has been read.
- Use the index on page 24 to select any pages to revisit.

The peaks are a harsh habitat, due to the cool, thin air and lack of food. There is little shelter.

Yet living things exist here.

In this habitat, living things must be good at looking for something to eat.

They need ways to adapt to the freezing surroundings.

Looking for a Meal

This bird has a long wingspan.
This helps it to stay high in the skies.

It spies a carcass and swoops down to feast.

9

From its lair, a big cat looks around for its next meal.

First it pursues a target
then it leaps to grab it.

This fox sleeps in the day, but must hunt during the day too.

It can hunt as a team.

Avoiding Being Eaten

This is like a rabbit but has round ears and a shrill squeal.

It has an underground den to shelter from hunters, like foxes.

Goats often stay high up to avoid hunters and look for food to eat.

They can leap and bound
on the steep cliffs.

The Himalayan marmot digs a deep den for shelter.

It has been hunted by humans for its thick fur and meat.

Humans in the Peaks

Living in the peaks is hard for humans too.

They may keep yaks for milk and meat.

Humans have found clever ways to exist in the bleak peaks.

Index